'When I first met Ian I was struck k
love for Jesus, his passion for the Cl
to his city! This engaging book reflec
Ian's call and purpose. These are not
but of a relentless activist as each pa   ... heat of the
author's heart. As you read you will discover that Ian is brave
enough, but the question that must be answered is, are we?'
Dr John Andrews (leader, teacher, motivator, author)

'I count Ian and Alyson as good friends and recognise them as a
couple of gentle provokers. You will find this book is filled with
a heart for unity, but also carries a fair amount of provocation
to think beyond our own paradigms. To get the best from it I
recommend we step back slightly and lay aside our defensive
mechanisms. The provocation is for purpose, and that purpose
lines up with the prayer of Jesus "that all of them may be one.
May they be brought to complete unity to let the world know
that you sent Me" [see John 17].'
*Stuart Bell (senior pastor, Alive Church, Lincoln and leader of the
Ground Level Network)*

'At the Evangelical Alliance we are passionate to see the great
John 17 prayer of Jesus outworked in the united mission of
God's people. *Are We Brave Enough?* is written out of Ian's
personal experience, his calling to Doncaster and the lessons
learned within One Heart One Voice, a unity movement
committed to transforming their city. There are parts of this
book which will leave you feeling uncomfortable; indeed, there
could be sections you disagree with, but let's allow the book to
challenge us to fresh steps of faith and obedience to the One we
love and serve.'
Steve Clifford (general director of the Evangelical Alliance)

'Ian and Alyson have served Doncaster over many years and
the results are visible. I have been to several unity events

organised by them over the last few years and it's been fantastic to see the way they gather people together to serve the agenda of transformation in the town. The recent Movement Day in Doncaster attracted not only the Church but also senior civic leaders. There was a real sense of shared purpose. They are brave and have inspired others to follow.'

Debra Green OBE (executive director, Redeeming Our Communities [ROC])

'Ian and Alyson's love of Doncaster is evident the first time you meet them. As part of the Church in Doncaster, they have a huge desire to see the Church being and working as one, to affect each of the different aspects of the life of Doncaster. In this book, Ian sets out five points to help see this happen in Doncaster, but also in *your* place. This book needs to be read, prayed over and thought through. There is a challenge here to how we are all together being one Church in our places.'

David King (director of Kingdom Voice Ltd, ambassador for the GATHER network)

'Ian's visionary leadership is transforming his city. Upon meeting Ian, I was struck by his passion for the local church, his passion around the commissioning of empowered Christian leaders in service of their city, and for the unity of the body of Christ. This book is so timely as we move with God's Spirit, calling us to surrender our silos and agendas for the advancement of His kingdom. I believe this book will tug at the heart of every leader to clearly discern God's voice in answering the call to be an agent of unity and city transformation. Get ready to be forever changed!'

Rev Ebony S Small (consultant, speaker, director of Movement Day Expressions, USA)

British Library Cataloguing-in-Publication Data

A catalogue record for this book is available from the British Library.

This book and all other Instant Apostle books are available from Instant Apostle:

Website: www.instantapostle.com

E-mail: info@instantapostle.com

ISBN 978-1-909728-97-4

Printed in Great Britain

Dedication

To my wife, Alyson, my soulmate and journeying companion; to my amazing children Matt, Tom and Grace and their incredible life partners Lucy, Lois and Dorian.

Thank you for the help and hope that each of you pours daily into my life.

Contents

Contents

Foreword

Rt Rev Peter Burrows, Bishop of Doncaster

Over the years, I've read many books and papers about ecumenism and church unity, all of them appealing for the Church under God to be one. In the past twenty years or so, the theological and practical outworking of church unity has changed. Most of it is now rooted in exciting local initiatives where churches and people from different denominations and practices come together in God's mission.

When I came to Doncaster in 2012, I discovered that one of the leading lights in this local movement was Ian Mayer and his family. Ian is a true Christian who has the natural ability and passion to work across, and engage with, the kaleidoscope of churches that can be discovered in any large town or city. He is a deeply thoughtful and prayerful person who does not just theologise about church unity, but also puts it into practice on a daily basis. This has impacted significantly on the way others think about this key aspect of mission in Doncaster, but also in supporting the local community, especially those most vulnerable. Ian believes passionately in making disciples but also in the social gospel and the public space the Church can hold.

This is reflected in this book in which Ian offers a clear theological rationale for Christian unity, practical examples and realistic challenge to all who take ecumenism seriously. But it is also a book written in hope and faith. To ignore the challenge Ian offers is in effect to ignore the call of the gospel for us all to become one. In the Introduction, Ian reminds the readers that when people became part of the first-century Church, it was 'inclusive, immersive and life-changing'. If we take God's call and challenge to become one and in our unity make new disciples, we too will continue to discover that life is changed beyond expectations not just for ourselves, but for those who come to know Christ for the first time.

This book is, for Ian, deeply personal, and that is reflected in the way he writes and makes what he says accessible. This is not a weighty dispassionate tome for academics, and is all the better for that. It is based in the reality of our times and the challenges ahead for Christians. It's a down-to-earth, practical and heartfelt call to all Christians from all denominations to unite in Christ, to value difference, to love one another as Christ loves us and together to look for signs of the kingdom in our unity and outworking of it.

Nothing perhaps drives people from the Church more than them seeing Christians falling out among themselves. Ian asks the question: Are we brave enough? I hope that reading this book will make you bold, and, where we have been lacking personally and in our churches, that we will embrace Christian unity as an urgent mission imperative that has the power to transform the Church and the world in which we live.

Let people see Christians alive with the Holy Spirit and passionate about the things of God, because that's when they might just want to know more. We need not be afraid of the challenge Ian lays before us, because God is with us.

Preface

Alyson Mayer

We certainly thought we were cool back in the day! I'm sure there is a whole generation of us out there who donned the velvet jackets and cowboy boots, picked up their guitars and played 'His Banner Over Me is Love'! Our 'band' was called Unity, and in spite of the random fashion sense and tinny-sounding songs, God was doing something profound during those days.

He was sowing the seeds and laying the foundations for a work that would span decades.

Ian and I, along with my brother Richard, played and sang together in churches across the network of an embryonic unity movement called 'His Fellowship'. This was an ecumenical initiative which held meetings in Epworth, north Lincolnshire, and had connections with an organisation called Doncaster United Christian Fellowship (DUCF); this was later to become Mission Doncaster. Ian had grown up with a Methodist background, my brother Richard and I were members of an Anglican church and, even then, God was overlapping the hard edges of denominationalism. Richard and I remember our father, Paul Tucker, joining the DUCF team which put together, and hosted, church unity events. Most memorable was the Dick Saunders Crusade in Doncaster, where many people came to Christ, and a choir was born that continued for some years, singing with one heart and one voice of unity. Seeds were being sown, and God's kingdom was growing. As a bunch of youngsters, we were starting to pick up the call to jumble up the labels and beginning to build a picture for which only God held the blueprint. Together, we remain passionate about the call that God placed on us in the 1970s.

Since those foundational days, unity has always remained at our heart. There are so many people, also from those days, whom we are still connected or working closely with. We honour each and every one.

Once married, Ian and I relocated to Lancashire (Ian's work took us there) where we were members of St James' parish church, Clitheroe, of which Ian's uncle was rector. We learned so much during those days and gleaned treasure from sitting round the rectory table, listening to the relational stories of sapling unity within the town. One of the greatest pearls from Uncle Kenneth's lips was: 'Don't waste too much time on meetings. In the great scheme of things, they are all phooey!' This man believed in relationships, and knew the benefit of chats over coffee or a meal rather than spending endless hours on committees.

In the early eighties, with our then baby son, we moved to Nottinghamshire to a beautiful village called East Bridgford. It was not only Ian's work with Barclays Bank which brought about this move; there was also a profound sense of calling to this place of my birth. It was to become the start of a new chapter on the unity journey. We became involved in both the parish church of St Peter and the local Methodist church where my mother in previous years had played the organ. The village was and still is a vibrant community with lots of social activities. Our two small boys were never short of friends or fun!

It was here, however, that we began to see a 'disconnect' between the church and the community itself. We became friends with a couple who had become Christians at a Billy Graham rally, so the four of us, while maintaining good relationships with the Anglican and Methodist ministers and congregations, began to meet in our homes.

For six years we remained in East Bridgford, and they were truly happy days. The friends made are friends kept, and are as family to us. The village life was idyllic and I could have stayed there forever ...

Between 1987 and 1988 we started to hear the whispers of a call to Doncaster. At first I shut it out; I didn't want to hear it. It felt too much like 'full circle' as it was to go back to where we had begun. I cited Lot's wife in my argument against it, and ignored God for some months. Ian was hearing the same call, unbeknown to me, at the time, and settled himself with this prayer: 'If this is You, God, and Your will for us, You'll tell Alyson!' I was putting the boys to bed one night and I knew. Don't ask me how; I just knew that Doncaster was to be our new home and that I needed to begin to cut the ties from my beloved village.

At Spring Harvest in 1988, we were in the main meeting and the preacher was speaking from the book of Deuteronomy. He pointed directly across to Ian and me and said, 'You have settled long enough in this place, the time has come for you to pack your bags and travel north.' In October of that year, we moved to Doncaster where it had all begun, pursued the call and ran with it.

On a much more personal level, Ian and I consider unity to be crucial in our marriage. We would be hypocrites if we didn't, and are constantly under the grace of God as He holds us together, as well as our daily choice to be a 'cord of three strands' (Ecclesiastes 4:12, NIV).

Our children, now three remarkable adults, know us as unity lovers. As their mother, bringing them up, the boys often heard me say, 'We will not have Cain and Abel in this house,' when arguments ensued! Working through differences was of paramount importance to us and remains so. We are a diverse family with differing views, but we love each other and treasure mutual loyalty. In the same way, our children have grown up with a background of denominational neutrality, knowing that each and every church has its own uniqueness. They continue to hold the DNA of impartiality by seeing the Church, the body of Christ, as one.

This is no fairy tale! There is an equal measure of blood, sweat and tears involved in this supreme calling. No melodrama here, just the reality of a resistance to something so close to God's heart that He commands blessing (see Psalm 133). The call always remains the same: to bring our meagre offerings of five loaves and two fish to the picnic to feed the multitude.

We love the Church. It is God's hope for the world, and the bride of Christ. Since attending church as children, committing to Christ as teenagers and receiving the call as young adults, for us, the multifaceted Church of Jesus Christ has always been and remains a huge part of our lives.

This book has been written with the invisible ink of passion. It flows directly from the heart of a man who means every word that he writes. I can assure you that every page holds to the truth, is measured with grace, and is underscored with the gentle roar of a lion.

Introduction
#5 changes

How we start is not nearly as important as how we finish; if we hope to see our world change, then we have to start with ourselves.

It seems like I've been writing this book for many years – I think someone once said that there is a book in everyone. The narrative of this book is, of course, interwoven into our own personal story, but I guess that it all started with this thought: How can we release the *whole* Church as *one* church across a city? I think that this question is partly answered through church unity, but I do think that it's also answered through how we *do church* together, and how we *share faith* together.

I don't think that the world is looking for theology, doctrine or even religion. I think that the world is looking for hope. I think that when the world looks upon the Church, it wants the Church to answer the questions it's asking, not the questions the Church artificially creates; and most importantly, it wants to find hope in those answers. What are those questions? I think they are simply, what do you believe, why do you believe it, and what difference does it make? A Christian community that focuses everything it does and says around answering these three questions is a Church that the world will be drawn to, and be desperate to be part of.

When meeting other Christians for the first time, how often have you been asked, 'Which church do you go to?' It's the standard question, isn't it? It's a way of framing the new relationship, and placing that relationship in a box so we know exactly what kind of Christian the person is. The question should really be, 'How is my Christian family where you live?'

We're living in a time when we need to position ourselves, and the groups we lead, to be agents of hope; this means we will need to make some hard changes to the way we *practise our faith*, and the way we *proclaim our faith*.

Let's be honest, today the word 'church' usually means an organisational unit operating in a particular locality. We all know that the 'church' is the people, but do we actually translate that knowledge into practice?

In Acts 2:42-47 there are six verses that should be the gold standard of how we *do church*:

> And they devoted themselves to the apostles' teaching and the fellowship, to the breaking of bread and the prayers. And awe came upon every soul, and many wonders and signs were being done through the apostles. And all who believed were together and had all things in common. And they were selling their possessions and belongings and distributing

the proceeds to all, as any had need. And day by day, attending the temple together and breaking bread in their homes, they received their food with glad and generous hearts, praising God and having favour with all the people. And the Lord added to their number day by day those who were being saved.

In the first century, 'church' was all about who you were and who you knew. It wasn't a church that you went to; there were no spectators or audiences. This was a community that everyone belonged to, and everyone was drawn to. It was inclusive, immersive and life-changing.

As well as looking at the way we *do church*, we also need to examine the way we *share faith*.

Our faith message today somehow needs to be realigned with the method and message of Jesus; the way we speak out that message needs to reflect the narrative that we read in the Bible. In Matthew 28:16-20 we read about how the disciples are placed up a mountain, with Jesus, prior to going out 'making disciples':

> Now the eleven disciples went to Galilee, to the mountain to which Jesus had directed them. And when they saw him they worshipped him, but some doubted. And Jesus came and said to them, 'All authority in heaven and on earth has been given to me. Go therefore and make disciples of all nations, baptizing them in the name of the Father and of the Son and of the Holy Spirit, teaching them to observe all that I have commanded

you. And behold, I am with you always, to the end of the age.'

Being up the mountain with Jesus is the starting point. Personal devotion and prayer has to be the foundation of our message, because we are the message. Jesus never told us to make, or merely be, *believers* – he called us to be *disciples*. Why? There is a big difference between the two. Are we getting people to be disciples or just believers? Belief is a binary choice but discipleship is a behavioural choice. You can believe in something and actually do nothing about it. To believe in something takes no real effort, just a decision. To be a follower or disciple of somebody means you commit to be transformed into their likeness and live out a life that looks like theirs.

It's a fact that everything either flourishes or fails, depending on the leadership. Whether in a small organisation, or an entire city, leadership sets the culture. Get leadership right and everything else follows. If we are to have the biggest impact in our place, we need to ensure that we focus on the areas where the shape of our place is being formed, and the narrative is being written.

Although the title of this book, *Are We Brave Enough?*, is a question to Church leaders, I'm asking all Christians to consider doing five things that could change the landscape of local church and help us all become more effective in transforming our world:

- #1 Behave as if we are all one.

- #2 Make changes to our priorities.

- #3 Learn to follow the bigger picture.

- #4 Include everyone on the journey.
- #5 Start to build differently.

Over these chapters, I'll take a look at these important mindset changes that I believe need to take place in the hearts and heads of all Christians, but especially Church leaders.

I'm eternally grateful to all the leaders across all the places and projects that Alyson and I work with. The stories in this book are real, and I've included them because they highlight real working relationships, and they show how we can learn from each other, even when the going is hard.

This book is not about being critical or negative about today's Church, its style or its leadership. It's an honest challenge that's intended to help us all get back to where we should be. I hope it will leave you with a sense of expectation that we could see real change over the next few years. I don't have the answers, but I believe passionately that the Church is the hope of the world.

I am convinced that Church leaders need to face some hard questions and, as a consequence, make some hard choices. It's going to be a brave leader that does so. The title of this book, *Are We Brave Enough?* is actually twofold, as it has taken bravery to write it. Although we *all* have a responsibility to get this right, I can't apologise for focusing on Church leaders – after all, it is leadership that has the greatest influence in turning things around.

It is my hope that the stories I've included are supportive. They are where life happens and, for better or worse, they have contributed to my journey. I think it's important that we model honesty and transparency, and that we are real about some of the challenges that come with leadership. I had to draw the line between stories that would contribute positively to the points I'm trying to make and the stories that would not. I'm eternally grateful to Alyson, and to experienced ministers and friends who helped me to discern the difference.

Most of all, I want this book to be real, not just theory. My desire is that the conversation continues and that Church leaders begin to get to grips with the mindset changes I've highlighted.

If you are up for the challenge, if you would like to see change, if you believe that things could be better, then I simply ask that you identify yourself, and the Christian group you lead, with the hashtag #5changes.[1]

We are living in challenging but incredibly exciting times. I truly believe that just five changes in leadership thinking could transform the landscape of the local church, and help us all become more effective in transforming our world.

I don't have all the answers, and I don't pretend to have it altogether, but I believe passionately that the Church is the hope of the world, and as such we need to get it right.

Are we brave enough to at least continue the conversation?

We have to be.

---

[1] A hashtag is a really useful tool on social media websites and applications, especially Twitter, to identify messages on a specific topic, and takes the form of a word or phrase preceded by a hash sign (#).

#1
Behave as if we are all one

Whatever Christian expression you lead or belong to, or whatever gathering style you might prefer, what really matters is how much that expression relates to and connects with all the other expressions in your place.

I love the mathematical definition of unity: 'a quantity assuming the value of one'.[2] There is a sense here of defining 'quantity' in the singular, rather than in the plural. To identify and brand ourselves, we search desperately for the right adjectives to put before the word 'church', and yet there is really no need. Can you imagine the Church across a locality choosing to be identified in the singular rather than the plural? Every denomination, every stream and flavour saying, 'We choose to be known as one. We are the Church.'

Doncaster in South Yorkshire is the one of the UK's best-connected locations. It is served by the UK's newest international airport, is at the heart of the UK's motorway network and the East Coast Main Line runs through the

---

[2] https://www.thefreedictionary.com/unity (accessed 21st August 2018).

town's high-quality urban centre, with London only eighty-eight minutes away. Doncaster is the largest borough in England by geographic area, which also sees it benefit from a significant natural environment. Together with its surrounding suburbs and settlements, referring to Doncaster as a 'city' can definitely be justified, although it is actually designated a 'town'.

In 2012, over breakfast, the newly appointed Bishop of Doncaster asked me a question: 'Ian, what is your vision for Doncaster?'

My answer was this: 'My vision for Doncaster is that when people look at our city, they see only one church.' This answer, although unrehearsed, had been sitting in my heart since the late 1990s.

What would happen if we all worked together through shared relationships, with shared values and a shared vision? If we all found value in our relationships with each other, and this helped each of us to do what we do individually more effectively? We could all share our individual resources and, by sharing a central branding, we could also enjoy the benefits of being associated with one another's successes! What would such a church look like? Are we brave enough to walk a path like this? Is it even a choice?

Years of research have shown that our family, the Mayer family, is made of hundreds of parts, and scattered across many locations. Each element is different to the others, and no unit is identical or uniform. Each has its own identity and each stands alone. However, we all consider ourselves part of one family because we are all united under one name, 'Mayer'. It's been interesting as we have discovered the diversity and stumbled across new branches; our family has grown in size but still remains one.

Sometimes when we are trying to unpack the meaning of something, it is more helpful to describe what it is not. Unity is not uniformity or conformity. It's not about creating a structure that contains, restricts or controls. It's not even coming to a combined agreement on particularly difficult issues. Unity is simply a relationship. It's a way of standing with others, despite differences in substance and style, and saying, 'We are one'. We reside under one name, the name of Jesus.

In John chapter 17, Jesus lifted up His eyes to heaven and said, 'Father, the hour has come; glorify your Son that the Son may glorify you.' I love this phrase. It highlights three unifying principles for me. Jesus knew that this was His time, He knew that this was His purpose, and He knew why He had to do it. Knowing 'when, what and why' are the keys to realising our potential. They are unifying principles because they cement together all that we are called to do. Whether we are leading others or ourselves, knowing the 'when, what and why' unites us. It unites groups and it unites us as individuals.

Jesus' passion was to be glorified for one reason only: that the Father would be glorified through Him. He went on to pray that 'they may all be one, just as you, Father, are in me, and I in you' (verse 21). Jesus was one with the Father, and His desire is that the Church is one with Him. This relational element of unity is one with Christ and one with each other.

John 17 is referred to as the 'High Priestly Prayer'; it's one of the final exchanges that Jesus makes before going to the cross, and it encompasses such powerful unifying principles. Jesus continues His prayer, 'The glory that you have given me I have given to them, that they may be one even as we are one, I in them and you in me, that they may become perfectly one, so that the world may know that you sent me and loved them even as you loved me' (verses 23-24).

The 'they' He was referring to was, of course, His disciples, but He also refers to those who will follow His disciples. 'I made known to them your name, and I will continue to make it known, that the love with which you have loved me may be in them, and I in them' (verse 26). Jesus prays that this oneness would continue to be made known so that the love that exists in that oneness would glorify the Father. He prayed that all believers might be as one body through their relationship with Him and the Father in Him.

Oneness with each other and Christ are not optional. Being 'as one' is the desire of Christ. In separating, dividing and disputing, we throw doubts upon the oneness of the Christian faith and we take glory away from Christ. The world will not be persuaded by doctrine or good argument. It will not yearn for communion with the Father on the basis of well-argued theology. It will not turn from destruction to hope because of moral judgements and condemnation. The world will yearn for the Father when it sees a Church that is one with itself and one with Christ.

Unity is most definitely relational; it is prayerful and it looks outwards. It's not just about doing things together, and it's certainly not polite ecumenicalism. Although ecumenical movements and initiatives can be great foundations for doing things together, they are not the relational unity we are referring to here. I'm defining unity in this instance quite distinctively. Unity is rooted in Jesus' words in John 17. It's an attitude of heart that, in being relational, spills out across a locality. It impacts those who are involved in it and who join the journey, but more than that, it infects those around it. It changes communities and it feeds a growing Christian presence as it permeates localities. Unity should exist in ourselves as leaders and with the group we lead.

Back in the late 1990s, something extremely powerful happened in Doncaster. A small group of church ministers met together and committed themselves to pray regularly for each other and the town. The group wasn't the idea of a single person and it wasn't formed by a committee. It was sparked by a move of the Holy Spirit that touched the hearts of a few church leaders. Initially the group consisted of just eight ministers, from eight churches and five denominations, but today that group forms the core of a strategic network of more than eighty churches across the borough of Doncaster.

Admittedly, formality has been added to the group over the years, and now under the banner of Mission Doncaster (and One Heart One Voice[3]), this group

---

[3] During 2004 Ian and Alyson formed the One Heart One Voice network with a vision to specifically reach out beyond the core

continues to help local churches develop closer relationships, joined-up thinking and a shared vision for the city. Even with this added formality, the key point is that this group is still relational. It's not based on structure but on sacrifice and service. It's a group that acknowledges the complementary roles we have in our joint call to see God's kingdom come. There is a voluntary recognition and acceptance of each other as part of the wider body of Christ.

For around twenty years, Alyson and I have overseen Mission Doncaster (and the leaders' network One Heart One Voice). Recent years have seen the profile of One Heart One Voice become more significant locally within civic and community connections. Alyson and I have been privileged to spend many years supporting and growing unity locally, and that role sees us spend time with many of the church leaders involved in the network. We connect with a range of expressions, and we relate to a range of ministry styles. It's a real joy to witness the vibrancy and diversity of Christian expression across the area. We have the freedom to contribute to, and also benefit from, the different groups across the unity network. It's not always understood that this role is one of itinerant service and support, and it does not imply exclusivity to, or favouritism of, any single expression. Alyson and I honour the freedom we have to work across the network, and to develop and grow the wider unity movement. We are able to operate in this way because we have a strong, accountable base into which we are rooted.

Doncaster Ministers Prayer Fellowship group and engage with Church leaders across the denominational spectrum.

Our rhythm of worship and gathering also lends itself to this pattern as we are not confined to Sunday-only meetings.

It's a fact that although we hear many hours of sermons preached each year, we can recall very few. Having said that, I remember listening to a young preacher who told a story about a video he had seen online. He described how the video shows a group of children in India running a race. The children all have physical impairments that make the race a big challenge for them, but regardless, they all enter into the race enthusiastically. During the race, one young child falls. This happens just as one of the children is about to cross the finishing line. Looking back, the child about to finish returns to help the fallen child and, without exception or hesitation, every other child comes back to help him too. They all support the injured child, and help to carry him across the finish line.

We can learn so much from this story. One child took the lead in returning to the child on the ground, and interestingly it was the child who was about to finish first. Wouldn't it be amazing if church communities that were doing particularly well, in terms of growth, resources and finance, reached out to those church communities that were not doing so well? Sometimes it takes one leader to reach out first, to set the example for others to follow. This sets a culture of support and collaboration, but more than that it says, 'We are all in this race together.' Being in the race together is so important. We have a spiritual enemy that prowls around seeking to destroy relationships and prevent new birth. It can be so easy to become discouraged or give up all together. When we stand together, we stand taller and stronger.

It is also worth remembering at this point that we have an enemy who 'prowls around like a roaring lion' (1 Peter 5:8). The enemy does not like unity – Christ's mandate for the Church as seen in the Upper Room Discourse (John 13–17). We need to be aware that the enemy seeks to 'steal and kill and destroy' (John 10:10). Divisiveness is a great weapon for the enemy, and we should be constantly on our guard against it. It is as we follow Jesus' command to love each other (see John 15) that we show the world the true witness of God's love in Christ.

I believe cooperation and togetherness are embedded into our nature. It's the way God designed and made us. It's always a joy to celebrate with church gatherings across the network, experience their diversity, and be refreshed with stories like this being shared from the pulpit.

If Jesus was able to unite Himself with God, and totally sacrifice His own life, our challenge must always be to sacrifice ourselves to the will of God, and surrender entirely to the unity of the body of Christ.

If you are a leader on the edge of unity, I would say to you – don't be. Call someone, arrange a coffee, and get connected. It's an imperative that you will never regret. If you are a leader in the centre of unity, I would say to you – go and find a leader who isn't. Grow some new relationships, and be prepared to see amazing things unfold as you partner and grow together.

There is only one Church, and it is this one Church that Christ will be returning for.

Call to action

So, how can we present ourselves as one church? How can multiple Christian groups in various locations with multiple stakeholders be 'as one'? This section offers some reflections and activities to help you begin that journey. Someone has to make the move in these situations, so it might as well be you!

- Spend time in prayer, asking God for protection over relationships within your leadership (or peer) group. Ask God to reveal those relationships that may be vulnerable, hard-going or difficult to manage. Ephesians 6:12 says that our battle is not against flesh and blood, but against 'powers' and 'principalities' (NKJV). Pray around those areas where you feel there have been difficulties in the past. You can do this by walking through those areas in your mind, or even taking some time out to do a prayer walk in specific locations.

- Within a five-mile radius of your locality, make a list of all the Christian groups and gatherings that you are aware exist (it may be appropriate to choose another distance measurement depending on the topology of where you are located). Using a map to mark out the locations in relation to your own group may be helpful.

- Once you have completed your list, write down the name of the leader (or key influencer) in each group.

Begin to pray for each person, their family and their circumstances. Think about ways you could begin to relate to, and meet with, each of these people. How would you make the initial contact and what would you plan to say?

Be intentional with your list; try not to let anyone slip through or be left out.

#2
Make changes to our priorities

Being consumed with our own group, denomination or network only serves to contain and constrain; it doesn't help to grow and develop the kingdom of God across a city; in fact, it hinders and restricts growth.

What would you think is the greatest barrier to Christian unity across a city? Is it our different theological standpoints? Perhaps differences in doctrine or perhaps, quite simply, our different worship styles? I would suggest that while these issues may play a part, the biggest barrier is self-interest. It is self-interest that consumes us, and restricts us from fully connecting with the larger kingdom picture.

Self-interest is often disguised as, 'I'm needed in my church,' 'I need to prepare for Sunday,' or simply, 'I'm too busy.' Of course, we must all play our individual roles well, I get that, but those roles should and must be interconnected. After all, there is only one Church and we are all part of it.

At the back of their minds, church leaders often ask the question, 'What will our folk get out of this?' before committing their participation to the larger kingdom picture. Kingdom economics operate in reverse, so this question should be, 'How can our folk serve this?'

It is said that you can tell a person's focus and passion, not by looking at the way they spend their money, not even by looking at their friends, but by the way they spend their time. Looking at a person's diary reveals more about them than looking at their bank statement. You can support something financially from a distance, but when you give time to it, you become part of it. Unity is not a spectator sport.

In 2016 Mission Doncaster had the opportunity as a unity movement to take a team to a major global conference in the United States of America. The conference fee was being paid for by the hosts, and unity movements from up and down the UK were all being invited to take teams. The focus of the event was city transformation.

In Doncaster, church leaders who had previously attended a pilot event in London were very keen to be involved and to attend the event. Their view was that we should choose specific people, who we felt would be strategic to Doncaster going forward, and invite them to make up a Doncaster team. This was a great idea in principle and could have worked really well. In reality, what happened was that time dragged on and on, and despite opportunities at leaders' events, weekly prayer meetings, and emails back and forth, none of the leaders made any progress putting a team together.

Time passed, and there was growing concern by colleagues I was working with, at a national level, that

Doncaster would not be represented.[4] Alyson and I decided to offer the opportunity to the whole of the network, and to especially encourage younger leaders to be part of the group. This was in line with the national agenda and the event theme. We put together some media and publicity, and began to share the passion and vision of what we believed would be an amazing opportunity. After a few weeks, we had a confirmed team of seven all prepared to go to the USA, five of whom were millennials.

Transparency and honesty are the hallmarks of relational unity at this level. What's interesting is the narrow lens that often restricts leaders from seeing their own lack of action, especially when looking at the bigger national picture. When a stronger and more focused leadership overtakes, it is sometimes easier to excuse our failures by blaming the strength of others.

This opportunity was strategic and it was powerful. Leaders from across the world gathered for three days of connection, celebration, education and inspiration in the Jacob Javits Convention Center in New York City for Movement Day Global Cities. The Doncaster team prayed, cried, laughed and challenged one another, but ultimately we came away humbled, energised and inspired to work together to see change in our city. The conversation we started in New York was also the

---

[4] Ian is a consultant for the Evangelical Alliance, currently working as part of the Public Leadership team. His role includes growing, networking and resourcing strategic leaders across the United Kingdom.

inspiration for Movement Day London and Movement Day Doncaster.

Leaders are often given every opportunity to take a lead in the big picture – but they don't. Why? My view is that many church leaders are absorbed and distracted by organisational and personal pressures. I'm often conscious of the 'ABC' pressures – attendance, buildings and cash. Church leadership, especially in its institutional form, is hard. It requires complete focus and commitment.

Sometimes, I wonder 'What am I doing here? Is this all worth it?' In 1 Kings 19:9, at the start of Elijah's journey, the Lord speaks to him.

> There he came to a cave and lodged in it. And behold, the word of the LORD came to him, and he said to him, 'What are you doing here, Elijah?'

Is God asking you, 'What are you doing here?' Perhaps the unity journey is hard for you. The Bible is full of conflicts and struggles, but it's within those moments that we ultimately find our way, and God reveals His purpose for us.

Elijah is having a bad day. He's the only prophet left, his life is in danger, he feels completely lost and he's hiding in a cave, but God speaks to him. God gives Elijah direction for the kingship of two nations, the appointment of a prophet and the destiny of some very specific individuals. His bad day is the gateway to someone else's future.

I wouldn't want to be in any place doing this stuff other than Doncaster. Even in the hard times, and especially the times of conflict, the urge to run or hide can be overwhelming. But I know that deep down God is working out His purpose and it's never time to give up.

Throughout 2016 we were praying about connecting with churches that were on the very edge of unity in Doncaster. This included reformed evangelical churches, Catholic churches and churches of different ethnicities. Connections with these groups had been historically difficult, so when I received a phone call from a black majority church leader who asked for a coffee, I was keen to accept!

As soon as I met him, I was excited to see that he had been consumed with a passion for unity, and had felt that it was vital he made the connection with the unity movement. We chatted for about an hour as he told me about his background and his church.

His desire was initially to open up his pulpit to network leaders and then to begin creating solid relationships with members of the network. He committed there and then to the weekly prayer meeting, and also to attending events and to supporting projects financially. I visited his church and saw this passion for unity echoed among his congregation.

I asked him, what made the difference? Why did he call me? What changed in him? Why the sudden passion for unity? Surprisingly, it was a member of a council department who was assisting him with a funding application, who simply said, 'You need to be part of One Heart One Voice; they connect *all* the churches in Doncaster as one.' When the civic authorities are pointing the church to unity, something amazing is happening!

In Exodus 33, there is a powerful passage about 'The Tent of Meeting'. We see God's presence resting outside the camp, not inside. In fact, we see His presence resting in a place far off from the camp:

> Now Moses used to take the tent and pitch it outside the camp, far off from the camp, and he called it the tent of meeting. And everyone who sought the LORD would go out to the tent of meeting, which was outside the camp. Whenever Moses went out to the tent, all the people would rise up, and each would stand at his tent door, and watch Moses until he had gone into the tent. When Moses entered the tent, the pillar of cloud would descend and stand at the entrance of the tent, and the Lord would speak with Moses. And when all the people saw the pillar of cloud standing at the entrance of the tent, all the people would rise up and worship, each at his tent door.
> *Exodus 33:7-10*

It makes you think, doesn't it? How often are we locked into our own individual camps? What difference would it make if we all stood at our doors and watched for the cloud?

I believe this is a new picture of unity. It's a picture that starts outside the Church, with God's Spirit taking the lead, rather than us. The time for institutional Christianity and brand-building Christianity is over. There's a new kind of unity being inspired by the Spirit of God. The Church needs to catch on!

It's time to think together and to stand together, truly as one.

Call to action

So, how can we change our priorities? How can we make sure that we are not always focused on our own group, denomination or network? How can we help to grow and develop the kingdom of God across a city? This section offers some reflections and activities to help you prioritise in a new way.

- Open your diary (calendar or phone) and look at the coming month. Spend time in prayer, asking God to create opportunities for new connections during the forthcoming events, meetings and activities that are listed.

- Try to categorise the events into two separate lists. Taking all the activities that are related to Christian work or worship, divide them as follows: those related to activities being done by your own group, organisation or denomination, and those that involve other groups, organisations or denominations.

- Make a third list of all those events and activities that are not related to Christian work or worship in any way. This could include paid work, family, friends, community, etc. Spend some time praying for the people involved in this list. Picture their lives and places and how you interact with them. Pray for new opportunities and contacts with these people.

- In terms of all the time you have available, assess how much time is allocated to each of the three lists above. Draw a circle and divide it proportionally into three areas. Label them as follows: 'our church', 'other churches' and 'not church'. Spend time praying about the time allocation you can see in the circle.

Think about how over the next few months you can reprioritise your diary to give time to the relationships outside of your own church gathering, and particularly connect with those who are not part of any church expression.

#3
Learn to follow the bigger picture

Every movement needs vision and leadership, and someone needs to be at the sharp end; as part of that movement, good leaders are able to support and honour the bigger picture without feeling threatened or reduced.

It is not unusual for me to have regular lunches or coffee with church leaders. I value the fellowship and the 'Iron sharpens iron' (Proverbs 27:17) environment that such meetings with leaders always create. On one occasion it was more about touching base with a leader who was, in a sense, a little disconnected from our network. He had not been seen for a while at our weekly leaders' prayer meeting or our regular leaders' network days.

We started by catching up with news about our respective families and ministries and then began to touch on town-wide issues. It was clear that there was unease in our conversation and we quickly got to the root of the issue.

Over the years there have been a number of occasions publicly where my leadership of the network has been affirmed by other church leaders. This has been either subtly through prayer or directly during meetings and events. This affirmation bothered this leader. He needed to know how I felt about this. How did I see my role in the leaders' fraternal and wider network? Did I see myself as a 'leader of leaders'? Did I think I was an apostle? The answers to these questions were important. He also wanted to know if my reason for meeting with him was to persuade him to be more involved with the fraternity.

I began by outlining my thoughts about my position, thoughts that were not unrehearsed, as this was not the first time I had encountered questions of this nature. I explained that, in short, I was the person whose role it was to make sure that the fraternal and wider network was driven and grown. Owning and running an internet development company has meant that I have been able to develop new forms of communication and media that ordinarily would not have been available to a network such as ours. This technology has been used prolifically in helping connect and inform leaders. I had been mandated by church leaders from across the town some years before to carry forward the fraternity into what was then a new chapter, to develop, coordinate, organise, facilitate and drive unity and vision. It was not a role of authority or status, but one of service. It was – and is – a role that I felt called to by God; it was part of me and part of my passion.

Our network is an organic movement, rather than an organised structure. It is a Christian leadership network that says, 'We stand together'. Despite struggle, conflict and differences, we are committed to praying, growing, sharing, loving and, when appropriate, acting together. Inevitably it requires a driver; I feel extremely privileged to be part of it and I feel very honoured that God has placed me at the centre and cutting edge of how it operates and grows.

Questions like this from leaders excite me. As I mentioned, this was not the first time I had been asked about my role. The questions reveal much about the leaders who ask them. Nevertheless, my view is that the questions always focus me. They help me keep my eye on the kingdom, and in this sense, although sometimes uncomfortable, I value the opportunity to be shaped and sharpened by answering them.

We continued to chat through the nature of my work, and relief, enlightenment and peace seemed to come across his face. He began to realise that my meeting with him was not 'to persuade him to be more involved with the fraternity' or exercise any level of leadership or authority over him, but rather to show him the value I placed on his gifts, anointing and friendship. It was an acknowledgement of the fact that the fraternity needs him, and he needs the fraternity. As a church leader in the town there can be no escape from the joint calling we have.

Afterwards, I sat and reflected on the first time, many years previously, that I had encountered questions of this nature.

Shortly after taking on the leadership role within the fraternity, I arranged a leaders' network day. The event called together church and ministry leaders from across our town. I set the agenda and, along with others, shared the vision and a framework for the future. I remember the day very clearly. During the coffee break in the morning session, one of the church leaders came to me with some questions; questions that centred on my ministry and role. Clearly I was exhibiting a leadership role that he was not comfortable with and he was confused about the nature of my ministry. I had not encountered this before. I was shocked, but little did I know that I was in training for similar questions over the coming years. From the outset I knew that God was doing a work within me and within the fraternity, and that God was shaping us for the future.

Before starting the second session of the morning, I took a decision to give the leader (and his companion) the floor. It was a big risk, but I wanted to submit to God's purpose. I introduced the leader, outlined his concerns and allowed him to speak to the fraternity. I was amazed at the response. The rest of the session was devoted to outworking my mandate and what my role meant for us as a group. I felt so affirmed and so blessed to be standing with such men and women of God as they grappled with the questions on my behalf. So often it's more about what others say and do on our behalf that speaks volumes.

I love the Greek word *hupotasso*; it appears around forty times in the New Testament, and is most famous for its blunt translation as 'submit' in Ephesians 5:22 when referring to wives and husbands. The term actually means 'to yield', and it has its origins in military strategy, meaning to 'arrange ... in a military fashion'.[5] There is significance here in terms of being arranged effectively.

[5] https://www.biblestudytools.com/lexicons/greek/nas/hupotasso.html (accessed 21st August 2018).

Are we prepared to fall into line for the sake of a greater and combined strategy, or do we always need to be 'top dog'? We need to work on the concept of mutuality and reciprocation in leadership relationships. I believe that when we learn how to follow in this spirit, then God can truly arrange us for His kingdom purposes.

Thankfully, over the years I have met very few leaders who struggle with the unity walk; most have broken through and have been prepared, to an extent, to walk the road. Unity is a path of being drawn together. It's a path of relationship and trust that reveals agreement and then action. It is about interdependence rather than independence and it culminates in blessing.

Working practically together in unity can be hard, and organising events and projects requires a level of give and take – success, however, must be based on core leadership relationships. Compromise and working around common denominators are usually prerequisites for success. Bringing together diverse and often opposing streams is a challenge, but it is possible if the 'table' is at the centre rather than the 'food'. Let me explain.

When our family comes together for food, we all like different things. There is much discussion about what we will eat. Some prefer Indian takeaway, others Chinese, others would love fried chicken! Whatever the preference, we are all agreed that the most important thing is that *we gather* and *we eat*. Getting universal agreement usually means that the traditional roast dinner wins the day – a favourite here in the UK. There is a message here. This is not about agreeing on the lowest common denominator, or settling for second best – the traditional Sunday roast is certainly not that! It is the coming together and the act of eating that is important. There is no place for a leadership narrative that promotes the idea that some church groups are ahead of others in hosting or culinary expertise!

In Luke 9:10-17 there is a story about food with which we are all familiar. Jesus is faced with the challenge of feeding everyone in a huge crowd, but He has only the limited resources that the disciples present to Him:

> But he said to them, 'You give them something to eat.' They said, 'We have no more than five loaves and two fish – unless we are to go and buy food for all these people.' For there were about five thousand men. And he said to his disciples, 'Make them sit down in groups of about fifty each.' And they did so, and made them all sit down. And taking the five loaves and the two fish, he looked up to heaven and said a blessing over them. Then he broke the loaves and gave them to the disciples to set before the crowd. And they all ate and were satisfied. And what was left over was picked up, twelve baskets of broken pieces.
> *Luke 9:13-17*

There is a beautiful picture here of unity, where everyone gets to eat because the food is shared as part of a giant picnic. Because the disciples shared and worked together, everything that was brought to the picnic was multiplied! There was more than enough to feed those who were there, and enough left over to give away. Isn't that what church should be, a giant picnic? Shouldn't church be where all of us bring our part, and play our part?

My heart is, and always will be, to support church leaders and to help gently reveal the blessing and power of unity. United leadership is more than just doing things together. It's more than events and it's more than projects. It's about relationships that say we don't mind who gets the credit because we are committed to a kingdom purpose, and that purpose overrides our own egos and our own agendas. We are secure in God and we are blessed by being one, together.

Driving and growing a network of church leaders brings a privilege of objective insight into a range of leadership styles and a range of church expressions, which ordinarily I would not experience if I was only part of a single expression. This insight is a kingdom commodity that should be valued and shared in humility. It's available only because of service, and it's important that it is used only as part of that service. It's not an insight that has any authority or rights. Secure leaders who desire to grow are not afraid to tap into this insight and to allow their churches to benefit from its objectivity.

Over the years I have met many different leaders, some of whom have become great friends. Leaders continue to come and go, many connect in regularly with what we do, and admittedly a tiny minority plough their own furrows; even so, Doncaster is a blessed place to be. It's a place where a great many leaders pray, work and grow together. They exhibit a oneness that comes not from good organisation and structure, but from a shared vision, shared passion and shared purpose for the kingdom of God.

Call to action

Strategic vision requires clear and influential leadership to make it happen. Key influencers are needed to help build and grow kingdom movements that will ultimately shape a place. This section offers some reflections and activities to help you understand your place as part of a bigger kingdom movement.

- Effective leaders are able to walk alongside those called to lead the bigger picture without feeling threatened or reduced. Spend time in prayer, asking God to guide your leadership (or peer) group in stepping out from your own container and connecting into the larger picture within your locality. It may be that there is a vacuum in your locality, and it's a call that you, along with others, should consider.

- Here are a few questions for leaders, mostly rhetorical, but nevertheless useful in looking at how we can embed the bigger picture into the Christian groups and organisations that we are part of:

  o How are you making the Christian group you lead aware of the importance of unity within your locality?

  o What steps have you taken to embed into your internal leadership team meetings the unity that you as leaders are currently experiencing?

o What steps have you taken to embed into your gathered church meetings the unity that you as leaders are currently experiencing? And how are you promoting unity within your local area to your gathered church?

o How do you plan to promote the relationships and activities that you as leaders are specifically developing?

o How do you plan to grow 'Iron sharpens iron' relationships with your specific leaders in your group?

Have you ever encouraged members of your church community to visit other church groups? It's worth a thought, isn't it?

#4
Include everyone on the journey

For true unity to work, the leaders of all the individual church groups need to passionately celebrate unity on a regular basis with all their teams and members; it's no good being part of the bigger picture if you don't connect this with those you lead.

There is usually a significant difference between how leaders perceive things and how the folk they lead perceive things. We need to see this gap bridged, so that the church groups, and not just the leaders, take ownership of the vision, passion and momentum that we are seeing in unity movements.

In terms of the finance needed to sustain the unity network Mission Doncaster, it's been mainly the leadership events and larger gatherings that have provided a very small income, often covering just the hospitality and venue hire. Any shortfall or extra funding has been met through our business contacts, and also close supporters of our charity, Jubilee,[6] which was founded in 1999. Jubilee works in partnership with

---

[6] Jubilee is a charity founded and led by Ian and Alyson.

individuals, groups and organisations, as well as through denominations, Christian networks and churches. The Jubilee vision is to see people develop a meaningful and authentic faith in every sphere of their lives.

Mission Doncaster formally began in 1987 when it was registered as a charity. Between 2003 and 2005, Mission Doncaster began to struggle as an independent charity, so in 2006 it was rebranded and adopted as a project of our charity, Jubilee. On 5th March 2008, Mission Doncaster formally ceased to be registered as a charity, and was reregistered as a working name of Jubilee.

Since 2008, Mission Doncaster has been a project of Jubilee. The Mission Doncaster project management group is delegated, by the Jubilee trustees, to the Doncaster Ministers Prayer Fellowship, which includes other local influential relationships. Jubilee also facilitates the use of a separate (ring-fenced) bank account. This bank account is managed independently from the Jubilee account, using additional signatories, so the financial aspects of the unity movement are distanced from Jubilee. This is a process we put in place back in 2008, so as to maintain a healthy distance between the finances of our charity Jubilee and the work of the unity movement Mission Doncaster.

In mid-2017, I suggested to a few leaders that it might be a good idea if we were to encourage church organisations to give regularly to the unity movements' umbrella organisation, Mission Doncaster. If we could encourage ten churches to give at least £10 per month, for example, then we would be able to fund more free places at our leaders' events, and honour visiting speakers more appropriately. Simple maths meant that we could easily raise the finance to grow and develop the network.

In reality, I knew the finance would be forthcoming regardless of the church buy-in. Vision and passion attracts resources, and our experience over the last twenty years is that there has always been provision for kingdom vision. I think this exercise was more about providing an opportunity for churches to partner, take ownership and share in the blessing of what has become a growing and dynamic movement.

I drafted an email to ten churches that I felt might wish to invest in Mission Doncaster and specifically support part of the work. The ten churches were noted for benefiting from the unity events across the city. The email was checked by a couple of leaders, and I sent it out with a sense of expectation.

A few days passed, and without any reservation, one church replied to say their leadership was 100 per cent behind the unity movement and would begin a monthly donation of more than twice what we had hoped for!

A few more weeks passed and, one by one, the other nine churches responded and said they would consider the proposal, and would speak with their wider leaderships. Some asked for more information about budgets and vision, but all, with the exception of one that was going through a very hard financial challenge, were happy to consider the request.

Three months passed, and after a second follow-up email to the churches that were still thinking about the proposal, it became apparent that most leaders were struggling to table the idea with their wider leadership, or even promote the idea within their church groups.

You would probably picture at this point archaic church structures, with church councils and traditional committees, sat in dull meetings, and you are unsurprised that there was some difficulty getting agreement – not true! The age or tradition of a church group makes no difference to how responsive they may be or how they engage with the bigger picture.

I think there is a leadership narrative that sometimes looks upon members as a commodity, and I guess the word 'members' does imply membership. When we use terms such as 'our folk' or 'our church', then that sense of owning the group we lead damages our capacity and willingness to let go of people.

Holding people loosely while trusting them to remain loyal to a particular church group requires bravery. Encouraging folk to freely engage with a range of kingdom activities outside their church promotes a sense of including everyone in the unity picture.

I understand that there is a balance in creating a sense of belonging within church communities; however, we also need to create a freedom that says, 'Lift your eyes beyond our community, and look outwards towards the kingdom landscape.'

I remember meeting with a church leader who had been appointed to grow a new work. The church aspired to plant in a few different places; it had a modern businesslike structure, and was appealing to a younger congregation. Even so, it was extremely difficult to develop any form of working relationship, knowing that after an hour or so of coffee, connection and enthusiasm could be undone in a minute by its internal leadership machine.

I understand accountability, but accountability is about being completely responsible for what you do and being able to give a satisfactory reason for your actions. It's not about constantly checking in with others before acting, or democratising your leadership, and it's definitely not about doing what others would prefer you to do.

I'm not asking leaders to be autocratic; I'm asking leaders to have passion about the bigger picture. I'm asking leaders to make the bigger picture a natural part of their internal structures and agendas, totally embedding the priorities internally. When leaders lead, people follow. Leaders don't need to present ideas positively; their passion and vision infects those around them and others sign up, sometimes with reservation, but nevertheless, they sign up and follow.

In Genesis 7:2-15 there is a story which, on the surface, is a recipe for disunity and absolute chaos. God tells Noah to collect in the ark all the opposites … Then in verse 16 we read that God shuts them in for 150 days!

> And those that entered, male and female of all
> flesh, went in as God had commanded him.
> And the LORD shut him in.

Richard Rohr, in his book *Things Hidden*[7] says, 'The ark is an image of the People of God on the waves of time,

---

[7] http://www.spiritualityandpractice.com/book-reviews/excerpts/view/18341 (accessed 21st August 2018).

carrying the contradictions, the opposites, the tensions and the paradoxes of humanity.' He goes on to say, '[The] gathering of contraries is, in fact, the school of salvation, and the school of love. That's where it happens, in honest community and committed relationships.'

I believe that we perfect unity among contradictions and contraries, and as we do so, we display hope to a watching world.

How did Noah do it?

> Then the LORD said to Noah, 'Go into the ark, you and all your household, for I have seen that you are righteous before me in this generation. Take with you seven pairs of all clean animals, the male and his mate, and a pair of the animals that are not clean, the male and his mate.'
> *Genesis 7:1-2*

There are two learning points here: firstly, we see how very different beings, with very different needs, can exist together, even when in a closed and confined space. Secondly, I believe that unity and transformation is possible within communities when we see a higher ratio of those who lean towards good than those who are opposed to good.

During 2018, as part of Movement Day Doncaster, Alyson and I had a conversation with the Bishop of Sheffield and the Bishop of Doncaster regarding church attendance for the Church of England in South Yorkshire and the East Riding. It transpired that the diocese had figures that stated on any given Sunday (2016), around 1.3

per cent of the population attend a Church of England church community. I remember the passion with which both bishops said that if we take all Christian communities in the same area, then the figure is nearer 4 per cent. How powerful it is when senior leaders look at the whole, rather than just their part. Imagine the force for change that the whole Church could be if we stood as one unit, and celebrated as a single brand.[8]

We need to learn how to be at peace with each other even when we hold issues unresolved and without perfect closure or explanation. I like the idea of a baton that's used in a relay race – passing on the vision to those we are leading and ensuring that unity is embedded into the fabric of our Christian community.

This mutual deference could actually be called 'forgiveness'. I believe forgiveness is the currency of unity and hope. Forgiveness brings reconciliation, reconciliation brings peace, peace brings unity, and unity brings hope. We perfect unity through relationship, and we display hope through that unity.

We are naturally drawn towards absolutes, conclusions and statements of agreement. We search for answers and outcomes, but hope doesn't reside in absolutes.

[8] Movement Day Doncaster,
https://vimeo.com/album/5253132/video/276915130 (accessed 21st August 2018).

Love is learned in the encounter with 'others' as Emmanuel Levinas taught.[9] Encounters with those not like us.

In Romans 8:24-25, Paul says:

> For in this hope we were saved. *Now hope that is seen is not hope.* For who hopes for what he sees? But if we hope for what we do not see, we wait for it with patience.
> (emphasis mine)

I believe hope is displayed in unity. The Church, as it models unity, displays hope.

Working with a neighbouring church you get on with is partnership, as is working with churches within your own stream. Partnerships are good, and can be fruitful, but we need to look beyond partnership. We are looking at a unity that is prayerful and relational, and reaches out way beyond our comfort zones, often connecting with those who are not like us – not like us at all. I like the idea of a five-mile mandate, where all the church groups within five miles of each other are compelled to work and grow together, where their leaderships meet regularly together and their congregations interact seamlessly.

Mission Doncaster has been a key part of the GATHER network for a number of years. GATHER exists to support expressions of unity across the country in cities and towns. GATHER connected with Movement Day in

---

[9] A Jewish philosopher whose world view was formed by the Bible; 1906–95.

New York and found that God was doing the same work of growing unity movements all over the world.

As I've mentioned, in October 2016, Mission Doncaster was privileged to be part of the UK group where leaders from across the world gathered for three powerful days of connection in the Jacob Javits Convention Center, New York City, for Movement Day Global Cities. Movement Day UK was subsequently held in October 2017 in London, with a team from Mission Doncaster attending and helping lead the event, which drew more than 1,000 leaders from across the UK.

In June 2018, Doncaster was the very first city-based Movement Day outside of London to be held in the UK. Movement Day Doncaster was about continuing the conversation we started in New York, growing the global relationships we began with the New York City leadership team, and encouraging commercial, church, civic and community leaders in Doncaster to jump on board. Alyson and I feel really blessed to be part of such an amazing unity movement in Doncaster, and it was incredible to see hundreds of key influencers gathering in Doncaster's premier performance venue, Cast.[10]

My initial question to the ten churches mentioned earlier was not about the money; it was about the kingdom. It was about looking beyond our own agendas

[10] During 2018, Alyson and Ian reached a turning point, where they felt that their centre of gravity was shifting. For more than twenty years, by the grace of God, they had worked with congregational church leaders to grow and develop unity within the context of Mission Doncaster and One Heart One Voice. Their next chapter was calling them to be a catalyst for unity across the entire spectrum of place leadership.

and standing together for something far bigger than ourselves. Not being afraid that one person – or one church or denomination – may be elevated above another, but looking ahead at what could be.

How are you leading your church community? Are you leading them for the kingdom?

Call to action

It doesn't matter what size of group you lead, or who they are, there will always be a gap between the way you perceive things and the way the rest of the group do. If we are going to see our wider world changed, then we need to close this gap and see the groups we lead aligned with our vision, passion and momentum. Imagine a city where the church looked like one, spoke like one, and acted like one, and start to visualise it. How amazing would that be! This section offers some reflections and activities to help you connect with the wider Christian community.

- Look at the list you made earlier of different Christian gatherings within five miles of your locality. How can you exhibit oneness to a watching world? Think about what it is that unites you with the other groups who are close geographically. Try not to focus on those things that may have separated you in the past, but try to look beyond style and theology to what you could all declare together. Think about things that could help cement the relationship.

- Having done some of the groundwork in #1, begin to make contact with at least two other key Christian leaders or influencers. Your groundwork should have revealed if there are any existing relationships in the area already meeting together (it's important not to reinvent the wheel or to duplicate).

- Think about the different hospitality options you may have locally, especially those that are neutral. Set an initial context, perhaps relating to neighbourhood safety or community well-being. Arrange to meet and to share your heart for unity. The seeds sown in prayer make the ground ready for unity.

Once there is some momentum in your locality, it's important that the forum and connections don't default into a cosy leader's fellowship or, worse still, a committee. Focus on relational activities such as prayer and eating and drinking together.

#5
Start to build differently

When we examine Church traditions and structures that many of us have known since childhood, they are found wanting. It is not that the Church we know is insincere or wrong, but rather that it has mislaid something along its journey.

Much of today's Church is congregational in shape, with strong institutional traditions combined with powerful branding. We've spent too long erecting buildings and focusing on gathering crowds. We have been taught that healthy things grow, and we have believed a narrative that says we need to get more people into our gatherings. Many Church leaders have become obsessed with building bigger crowds. The real truth is that healthy things reproduce.

There are glimpses of exceptions, but mostly the Church today does not look like the Church that we read about in the book of Acts. How did we get to where we are now, and how can we pull things back?

A brief look at history[11] shows us that in the first and second centuries, the Christian faith had exploded, creating multiple communities across many locations, and by the third century, six million Christians lived in the Roman Empire alone. It is widely understood that in and around AD 300, Constantine noted the growing popularity of Christianity. He adopted the first two letters of Christ's name in Greek as a symbol to be used on the shields of his warriors and extended toleration to all Christians. During the reign of Constantine, Christianity was legalised by the Roman Empire, and would later become its official religion. In circa AD 326 Helena (Constantine's mother) made a pilgrimage to Jerusalem to find the relics of Christ's cross at the crucifixion site. Helena was instrumental in helping Constantine 'take over' Christianity. In AD 337 crucifixion was banned and Constantine was baptised just before he died.

At the end of the third century AD, the Church, which had initially gathered in homes, started to meet in dedicated buildings. From there, history reveals that pagan temples were converted into places of Christian worship, the Church becoming centralised and audience focused. This theatre-style design has remained as the predominant church format until this day.

By using purpose-built buildings and placing order and liturgy there, the very DNA of the Church was

---

[11] See: William A Beckham, *The Second Reformation: Reshaping the Church for the 21st Century* (Houston, TX: Touch Publications, 1995, 1996, 1997), pp41-50; Ralph W Neighbour, *Where Do We Go From Here? A Guidebook for the Cell Group Church* (Houston, TX: Touch Publications, 1990), pp11-37.

changed. The vibrant, disruptive and passionate Church that had emerged from the lives of the first-century Christians, and the message of Jesus, was now being subdued into a contained mechanism instead of a vibrant activist movement. The spiritual warfare element here reflects the fact that the enemy did not have the power to destroy the Church, but was able to disrupt and seduce it. There was a change in thinking about God's Church – as an organisation, rather than as an organism.

Since the third century many things have differed from church to church – theological interpretation, worship styles, building formats, etc – but a cathedral structure, congregational gatherings and a programme-based design has remained constant over the last seventeen centuries.

Throughout the history of Christianity there has been an unhelpful shift from being a radical political and spiritual movement to being seduced by a theatre-based model that craves crowds and applause.

So, how can we rediscover the passion and power that was clearly part of the early Church, 2,000 years ago? I like the contrast between the two words *organisation* and *organism*. Organisations are about being ordered; they are about creating structures through which individuals cooperate systematically to conduct a specific business. An organism, however, speaks about the various ingredients and processes of life, about being mutually dependent and essential to life.

What would a church that resembled an organism look like? I believe first and foremost it would be *indigenous*. We would see a total connectedness between faith, family, work and every other sphere of life. For too long we have divided the world neatly into two. One part is sacred, which involves all things Church, such as worship, Bible studies, fellowship, 'Christian work', etc. The rest of life has been described as 'secular'. This sacred and secular divide immobilises the Church in its mission to the world. In Psalm 24 we read, 'The earth is the LORD's, and everything in it, the world, and all who live in it' (NIV). Our faith is relevant in our household, neighbourhood, workplace and fellowship. The word 'indigenous' is all about living or occurring naturally; it's not about importing, but more about the native and innate. A visual picture of an indigenous church could be that of the contrast between that of a *plantation* and a *forest*.

Within the plantation, everything is controlled and sterile. Although plantations can often appear large and productive, there is very little spontaneous life. Security is in the order and routine. Within the forest, many different species exist together, working in harmony and being interdependent. Growth is spontaneous, unfenced and not controlled by humankind. The difference between that which is man-made and that which is naturally produced is evident all around us; we can see a clear contrast between humanity's order and God's order. Are we building plantations or growing forests?

I'm not trying for a moment to suggest that we should stop our congregational gatherings and all go back to a first-century model. Let's face it, that's not practical; lots of people enjoy the various congregational gatherings and styles. In recent years, multimedia-led gatherings, with professional bands and motivational speakers, have been successful in attracting large numbers of people. Although they tend not to shout about it, the more traditional, liturgical gatherings have also gathered large numbers; they offer something solid and timeless for those who are lost. What I am saying is that we need to be honest – these expressions are great, but they are not our home. Yes, it's an opportunity for God's people to pray together, praise together and hear from the Bible, but is it Church? I don't think it really is.

I ask this in the context of leading a unity movement that contains, on the whole, more than eighty congregational models of Church, and for the record I'm committed to seeing these expressions grow and flourish. However, we don't see this in the New Testament, and to make it our focus and to call it 'Church' is misleading.

We all know in our heads and hearts that, in the context of the New Testament, the Church refers to the people, the individuals who belong to Jesus and who are called to be in a relationship with Him and each other. Church can refer to all the followers of Jesus everywhere, or just those believers in a certain location. My challenge is this: although we know this in our heads and may even believe it in our hearts, what do we actually do about it? Are our actions rooted in this principle, or are we running away with building something else?

The Greek word *ekklesia*, which is often translated 'Church', is a combination of two Greek words: the Greek word *kaleo* (which means 'to call') and *ek*, meaning 'out' or 'out of'. Therefore, *ekklesia* is can be translated as 'called-out ones'. I think this describes us really well, as the called-out ones!

Alyson and I have been on an 'indigenous' journey since 1998, and accompanied by many, many friends and family, we are privileged to be able to lead a movement. When we founded Jubilee, our vision was to see people develop a meaningful faith in every sphere of their lives and be empowered to make a transforming contribution to society.

In 2014, we heard from God that we needed to expand and connect our journey with more of those who are outside any Christian gathering or context. Alyson felt God clearly say to her, 'Give them something to eat.' Food is a great connector. Eating together cements relationships and grows communities. It's interesting that the first-century Christian community was built around food and that food played an important role in the life of Jesus and His disciples!

As a result of God's speaking to Alyson, Manna Community[12] was born. Manna Community CIC[13] is all about supporting people on life's journey. We have a number of buildings – one café-style, workshops and counselling rooms, among other things – and we supply a range of services and provide events too. Manna's vision is to facilitate a space for meeting the broad range of needs within the local community: physical, intellectual, emotional, social and spiritual. By creating a professional café culture that can act as a context for meeting, we have been able to reach out to the community. Reaching out can mean a number of things. It can mean gathering those together who have suffered loss, providing food and

---

[12] http://www.manna.me.uk/cic/timeline/ (accessed 21st August 2018).
[13] Community Interest Company.

comfort and bereavement counselling. It can mean taking young people who have fallen out of school and helping them to find hope and purpose through alternative training opportunities. It can mean offering mentoring to business leaders. Or it can simply mean providing a Christmas lunch to the local children's services. However it happens, it always looks like community and hope.

As Manna Community has grown in influence and reach, it has been important for us to ensure we are identified as a Christian group. We understood the need to articulate what we believe, and to be able to state this clearly, while avoiding the usual pitfalls of jargon and theology. It wasn't easy, and it took a few months, but this is what we believe God wanted us to say:

> Here at Manna Community, what we do is very much motivated by our faith. It not only shapes the way we work, but it changes the entire way we live.
>
> Quite simply, we believe that our lives are being transformed through a conversation that started over 2,000 years ago. It's a conversation that began in the first century with a man called Jesus. Because of Jesus, we can understand more about God, and more about our relationship with God.
>
> The life and actions of Jesus inspire us and compel us to live and work as He did. Particularly the fact that His unconditional love for humanity was the motivation behind everything He did.

> At Manna Community we're all still
> having the conversation that Jesus started,
> we're still being transformed, and we're still
> discovering our place in the world.
>
> Today, Jesus remains the most influential
> and talked-about person in history. If you'd
> like to talk with us further about who Jesus is,
> and how you can learn more about Him, we'd
> love to meet with you.

This statement identifies Jesus as the central character in our faith, and it clearly opens up the conversation to those around us. Nelson Mandela said, 'If you talk to a man in a language he understands, that goes to his head. If you talk to him in his language, that goes to his heart.'[14] How we communicate our faith and how we celebrate our faith are crucial to how engaged we will be with a watching world.

I believe that through Manna Community, and groups like it, we are undergoing a restoration, or rediscovery; we are slowly uncovering what has been hidden, overlaid and forgotten. We are restoring the principal structure of the Church – an indigenous Church that demonstrates Christ to the world by demonstrating the qualities of Jesus.

In Acts 2:42-47 we read about 'The Fellowship of the Believers' in some detail. It's only six verses, but it's packed with a wide range of activities and attitudes that are the hallmark of the early Church.

---

[14] http://www.bbc.co.uk/worldservice/learningenglish/movingwords/s hortlist/mandela.shtml (accessed 21st August 2018).

And they devoted themselves to the apostles' teaching and the fellowship, to the breaking of bread and the prayers. And awe came upon every soul, and many wonders and signs were being done through the apostles. And all who believed were together and had all things in common. And they were selling their possessions and belongings and distributing the proceeds to all, as any had need. And day by day, attending the temple together and breaking bread in their homes, they received their food with glad and generous hearts, praising God and having favour with all the people. And the Lord added to their number day by day those who were being saved.

Marcel Proust once said, 'The real voyage of discovery consists not in seeking new landscapes, but in having new eyes.'[15]

Built on the principle that all Christians are ministers, we should actively seek to develop each disciple into the likeness of Christ. This is where love, community, relationships and ministry spring up naturally and powerfully. Discipleship starts the moment we meet someone. The life of the Church is in people, not in buildings or programmes. The primary building blocks of the Church are its people, and the Church should be a kingdom organism that grows people and reproduces.

[15] https://www.brainyquote.com/quotes/marcel_proust_107111 (accessed 21st August 2018).

The Church is a dynamic, organic, spiritual being that can only be lived out in the lives of believers in community.

The first-century Church and the twenty-first-century Church are completely different in shape and focus. It really is time for us to take a fresh look at what we currently know as 'church' and to uncover what has been lost and hidden.

The kingdom of God advances at the speed of relationships, and as leaders our role is to provide contexts for those who are connected with us to grow and flourish. As Christians there are two clear elements to our call: 'Love the Lord your God with all your heart and with all your soul and with all your mind ... love your neighbour as yourself' (Matthew 22:37-39).

We reproduce what we are. It really is that simple. I know that it's not possible to go back and change the beginning, but we can start where we are and we can try to change the ending.

Be honest with yourself: are you building a machine, or a movement?

Call to action

The Church is a collective of all those who declare to follow Christ, who have committed to be like Christ and are distinctive in the world because of Christ. This section offers some reflections and activities to help you take the lid off your church gathering, and rediscover what it really means to be Church.

- Think about what your gathering could start to look like if it changed from a congregation to a conversation. Spend time in prayer asking God to help you look at your church community in new and creative ways. In John 18:37 we read that 'Everyone who is of the truth listens to [Christ's] voice.' What opportunities are there within your gatherings to listen to the voice of Christ? Do you need to make space and time for your church community to rest in His presence and hear His voice?

- Does your church gathering mostly all face the same way, listening to the same thing at the same time each week? How many opportunities are there within your gatherings to have conversations with those who are both inside and outside the church community? Many church communities are based on a club style, with a membership approach. How could your church group look if you were to focus on conversations and stories?

- When was the last time you cancelled your main gatherings in favour of asking your church community to spend time with their families and neighbours? What would you do to make this happen?

What would happen if we were to move out of our routines into relationship-based gatherings? Over the next few months, look at how you can spend time outside your church groups. Always keeping Jesus in the centre of your life, lean outwards, along with others, into the world and be prepared to be amazed.

Conclusion

With all the various streams and flavours of Christianity, all professing to know the truth, how can we possibly know what's right?

I've been asked, 'Are you a Christian?' by all kinds of people, and it's often followed by, 'What kind of Christian are you?' This is a question I love to answer because it relates directly to what I believe, why I believe it and what difference it makes in my life. It's a question that opens up a conversation and allows me to learn more about people and their needs, and ultimately it opens up relationships.

The dictionary definition of 'Christian' can be paraphrased along these lines: 'relating to, or professing Christianity or its teachings, having qualities associated with Christians, especially those of decency, kindness and fairness.' Although this is a good starting point, it tends to fall short for two reasons. Firstly, what are the 'teachings of Christianity'? Let's face it, even Christians have difficulty coming to an agreement on this! Secondly, there are many, many people who declare themselves *not* to be Christian but are 'decent, kind and fair'.

An alternative dictionary definition might be: 'a person who has received Christian baptism or is a believer in Christianity.' Again, this is tricky, because we all know people who tick these boxes but, in practice, we know in our hearts they are far from being 'Christian'.

So what is a Christian? Whenever I look at the cross, I'm reminded of a time, as a young teenager, when gazing upon it changed my life forever. How we see things matters. Is the cross simply a symbol of torture and death, or, as I found out more than forty years ago, is it a symbol of hope and life?

Today, each time I look at the cross, I see my life through that lens of hope. I'm put into the context of eternity, and I'm instantly connected with a God who cares about me and desires the best for me.

That profound encounter during those confusing teenage years brought about a perspective that changed my life and transformed my thinking forever. It was a pivotal moment where everything changed. My life and purpose would never be the same again.

Having been brought up in a Christian home, I'd seen the cross many times and I thought that I understood its symbolism, but I knew deep down that my life still lacked meaning and purpose. I had some great foundations, but I needed to know what the cross meant *for me*.

For as long as I can remember, I have been in conversation with God. When I was a very small child, my aunt bought me a Bible. In the front she had written, 'For God so loved Ian that He gave His only Son that if Ian believes in Him, he shall not perish but have eternal life.' In those first few years, this verse set in motion a desire to have a conversation with the divine that was personal to me.

What set Jesus apart was not just His life, but His death too. I knew in my teenage years that my decision to follow Him and to allow Him to shape my life was either the most important thing I would decide, or it didn't matter at all. In life there are some decisions that matter, and there are other decisions that do not. This decision was one that mattered. I realised then that Jesus was the lens through which I could begin to understand the world around me, and my place in that world.

This man who chose to go to the cross did so for me, and 2,000 years on I would be able to partake in an amazing relationship with God, and also experience the restorative nature of God because of Him.

The Good Shepherd

I really love the picture of the Good Shepherd that we read about in John 10:11-18:

> 'I am the good shepherd. The good shepherd
> lays down his life for the sheep. He who is a
> hired hand and not a shepherd, who does not
> own the sheep, sees the wolf coming and
> leaves the sheep and flees, and the wolf
> snatches them and scatters them. He flees
> because he is a hired hand and cares nothing
> for the sheep. I am the good shepherd. I know
> my own and my own know me, just as the

Father knows me and I know the Father; and I lay down my life for the sheep. And I have other sheep that are not of this fold. I must bring them also, and they will listen to my voice. So there will be one flock, one shepherd. For this reason the Father loves me, because I lay down my life that I may take it up again. No one takes it from me, but I lay it down of my own accord. I have authority to lay it down, and I have authority to take it up again. This charge I have received from my Father.'

You get the idea from the title, and use of the term Good Shepherd, that there were also bad shepherds!

The shepherd carried a number of important tools; for example, a sling, a staff and a rod. For the shepherd the sling had two purposes: to *guard* and to *guide*. Because the first-century shepherds did not have dogs to send after a straying sheep, they would often use their sling to drop a stone in the path of a wandering sheep, warning them and helping to guide them along the right path. The shepherd also carried the staff in his hand when he walked; it was a long stick, with a large curved hook on the end. When a nearby sheep showed signs of straying, the shepherd would reach out and gently pull it back. The rod, which I imagine was like a short club, was probably carried in the shepherd's belt.

The first-century shepherd had a deep love for the sheep in his flock, and a self-sacrificing spirit. Every evening, the shepherd would gather the flock into the fold, a corral made from stones or bushes clumped together forming a large circle. All the sheep had to enter the fold through a narrow entrance, and as they came in, the shepherd stretched his long staff across the entrance, close to the ground, making each sheep pass 'under the rod'. As each sheep passed through, the shepherd gave it a quick examination to see if it had suffered any injury during the day. This is the picture Ezekiel gives of God's loving care for His people, when the prophet hears God say, 'I will make you pass under the rod' (Ezekiel 20:37).

Once the flock was safely inside the fold, the shepherd would lay down across the entrance so no sheep would get out, and no threat could enter without passing over the shepherd's body. In this way, the shepherd literally became a protecting door to keep the flock safe. It's no wonder that Jesus adopted the picture of the shepherd and made it a portrait of Himself. And of course, God is referred to as the 'shepherd' in the Old Testament – for example, Psalm 23; Isaiah 40; Ezekiel 34:15 – and His people as 'sheep' (see Psalm 79:13; 95:7; 100:3). There is also a messianic connection; for instance, see Ezekiel 34:23, Micah 5:2-5.[16] Jesus, by using the term, was clearly identifying Himself with God ... and as Messiah.

God's restorative love

I don't believe God has a big stick and is out to get us. I believe He's a God who knows each one of us intimately – whether we speak to Him every minute of every day or

---

[16] For God's people as straying sheep, seeing Isaiah 53:6.

whether we ignore Him, His love still reaches out to us. Ultimately, 'God is love' (1 John 4:8), and this is the central message of the Bible. Any theology, doctrine or narrative that says otherwise is simply not from God.

In Matthew 22, Jesus is questioned by the religious leaders of the day:

> But when the Pharisees heard that he had silenced the Sadducees, they gathered together. And one of them, a lawyer, asked him a question to test him. 'Teacher, which is the great commandment in the Law?' And he said to him, 'You shall love the Lord your God with all your heart and with all your soul and with all your mind. This is the great and first commandment. And a second is like it: You shall love your neighbour as yourself. On these two commandments depend all the Law and the Prophets.'
> *Matthew 22:34-40*

The question is asked by a lawyer, and the whole tone of the passage is an attempt to catch Jesus out by exposing His interpretation of the Scriptures in a negative way. What actually happened was that Jesus gave a reply that could not be refuted; reading further, Jesus addressed the whole issue of His own relationship with God (verses 41-45), and therefore His authority to teach and speak about God as He did. No one was able to answer Him back, 'nor from that day did anyone dare to ask him any more questions' (verse 46).

It's entirely possible to interpret the Bible in a transactional or absolute way, and then exclude others who have alternative interpretations on a range of issues. For example, whatever your views may be on church leadership, gender, baptism, the Holy Spirit, Israel, sexuality, the end of the world, etc, these views are not nearly as important as the two commands that Jesus says are central to the Bible, and central to being a Christian.

I'm not saying that specific opinions and views on such subjects should not be held, or that certain views should not be promoted or defended. What I am saying is that no single viewpoint makes you Christian or discounts you from being a Christian. There is no set of absolute opinions or viewpoints based on these disputable matters that constitute the definitive Christian message. The definitive message of the Bible is love and grace – any message that distracts us from this is not the message of Christ.

I love the conversation recorded in Luke 23 that takes place with Jesus and one of the criminals on the cross beside Him:

> One of the criminals who were hanged railed at him, saying, 'Are you not the Christ? Save yourself and us!' But the other rebuked him, saying, 'Do you not fear God, since you are under the same sentence of condemnation? And we indeed justly, for we are receiving the due reward of our deeds; but this man has done nothing wrong.' And he said, 'Jesus, remember me when you come into your

kingdom.' And he said to him, 'Truly, I say to you, today you will be with me in Paradise.'
Luke 23:39-43

There is no specific 'sinner's prayer' here; there are no tick-box steps to salvation or a set of doctrines to sign up to; there is just a simple cry to Jesus for restoration. What would happen if all anyone needed to do was cry for help, and Jesus was there? I believe that a message of love makes that possible through believers like you and me.

Journeys and transformation

Every journey has a starting point and every transformation has to begin somewhere. I was brought up a Christian; I spoke like a Christian and acted like a Christian. In 1977 I went away on a New Year Inter Schools Christian Fellowship weekend. On the New Year's Eve, I realised that if the message of Jesus was true and relevant, it had either to be the most important thing in my life, or it didn't matter at all – there was no in-between. That night, I made a decision to put Jesus at the centre of my life, to follow His example and to allow Him to shape me. My parents recall that on my return, there was a difference – I had changed.

Although my journey began in 1977, there have been many pit stops, refuelling opportunities and revelations that have shaped me and equipped me.

In 1998 God began a new work in us as a family. Alyson and I stepped out of congregational church and began a journey with our three children. We reformatted our lives to develop a total connectedness between faith, family, work and every other sphere of life.

There are lots of different ways of understanding journeys and working out where people are on their own journey. The Engel Scale was developed by James Engel as a way of representing the journey from no knowledge of God (-8) through to spiritual maturity as a Christian believer (+5). The model is used by some to emphasise the process of 'conversion' and the various decision-making steps that a person goes through before they truly come to faith. The model was developed mainly by Engel, who used several ideas from behavioural science practices; he then published it in his 1975 book, *What's Gone Wrong With the Harvest?*[17]

In our business consultancy context we use a scale to assess potential customer engagement. DAGMAR (Defining Advertising Goals for Measured Advertising Results) is an advertising model that was developed by Russell Colley in 1961 and is used in business promotional strategies. According to this model, which was developed to measure the effectiveness of advertising strategies and examines the potential customer's state of mind, there are four stages of thought: awareness, comprehension, conviction and then action. It encourages advertisers to think about the target recipient of the message, and what the advertiser is aiming to achieve through that message.

So, as Christians, we need to consider our 'audience' and the goal of our message. It's not enough to just say

---

[17] Grand Rapids, MI: Zondervan.

our audience is the 'unsaved' and our message is 'salvation'. We need to be more intelligent and more intentional about how we connect a searching world with the message of Jesus. After all, the message of hope that Jesus brings is not a product, the church is not a business, and we're not looking for customers!

As I have mentioned above, we tend to view the world in two separate compartments: sacred and secular. We do evangelistic sorties in attempts to grab people, and try to pull them from the secular to the sacred. But the Christian life is one of relationship, not just a set of principles and processes.

Lessons from Zacchaeus

So, all of humanity is on a journey through life. The story of Zacchaeus in Luke 19:1-10 is a journey that takes place in the heart of one man. I think we can learn a lot from each step on Zacchaeus' journey, not only for our own journey, but also as we reach out to others:

> He entered Jericho and was passing through. And there was a man named Zacchaeus. He was a chief tax collector and was rich. And he was seeking to see who Jesus was, but on account of the crowd he could not, because he was small of stature. So he ran on ahead and climbed up into a sycamore tree to see him, for he was about to pass that way. And when Jesus came to the place, he looked up and said

to him, 'Zacchaeus, hurry and come down, for I must stay at your house today.' So he hurried and came down and received him joyfully. And when they saw it, they all grumbled, 'He has gone in to be the guest of a man who is a sinner.' And Zacchaeus stood and said to the Lord, 'Behold, Lord, half of my goods I give to the poor. And if I have defrauded anyone of anything, I restore it fourfold.' And Jesus said to him, 'Today salvation has come to this house, since he also is a son of Abraham. For the Son of Man came to seek and to save the lost.'

Journeys are gradual and incremental. I see six waypoints in Zacchaeus' journey that can teach us about how others can connect with Jesus. (It is generally understood that a waypoint is an intermediate point or place on a route or line of travel, a stopping point, or point at which course is changed.)

1. He was challenged; everyone is looking for something, but they often have challenges within themselves or from others (or a combination of both) that prevent them exploring and going deeper into what really matters. Here Zacchaeus was held back by both, see verse 3.

2. He was compelled; something within Zacchaeus made him act. He ran and climbed. I see a world full of those searching for hope and compelled to find it. To 'compel' is really about having an irresistible effect, a

powerful influence. That's the Jesus that I know – He compels us all to know Him more. See verse 4.

3. He was connected; Jesus connected directly and deeply with Zacchaeus. He was intentional and He was relational – verse 5.

4. He was criticised; there will always be those who criticise. Those who are jealous or locked into their own ideologies or theologies – how can Jesus be a guest of a sinner? See verses 6 and 7.

5. He was changed; connection with Jesus ultimately changes people. It affects them on every level. It's not a one off event, or a transaction, it's a process and relationship. Verse 8.

6. He was celebrated; we need to celebrate the lives and journeys of those around us. Some may be moving towards Jesus, some may not, but either way, let's celebrate each other, and connect. Verses 9 and 10.

In just ten verses, the story of Zacchaeus shows us the simplicity of this 'salvation' journey. Being a Christian is about aligning ourselves with Jesus and allowing Him to change and restore us. When we are in relationship with Him, we produce fruit, and we stand out as distinctive people in the world.

So often in church gatherings we see a focus on a transactional salvation and we develop a narrative that reduces the message of Jesus down to a single act: conversion. The result is a gathered church that makes conversion of the lost its mission. Salvation is far more than this. It's a restorative journey; and as we read the

Bible together, facilitated by the Holy Spirit, this journey is outworked in a conversation with Jesus and each other. The conversation is the mission, and it's this mission that creates the church. The message of the Bible is simple: love God, love each other and love ourselves.

Humanity has been searching for a way back to God since we walked with Him in the Garden and then walked away. Jesus opened up that conversation between humanity and divinity, and in it revealed both the relational and restorative aspects of the divine. Without Jesus, any theology, doctrine or ideology is empty, it lacks eternity – remove Jesus, and you remove meaning and hope.

As for me, I'm still having the conversation I began back in 1977; I'm still being restored, and I'm still discovering my place in the world.

Prayer

If you would like to take a step towards God, it's really easy. All you need to do is pray. Prayer is simply talking to God. Let me help you ...

Almighty God, creator of heaven and earth,

I am empty, lost and broken, and I don't know which way to go next. Help me to reconnect with You, and forgive me for the things I've done which I know in my heart are wrong. I look to You for direction, hope and restoration. I believe that if I place my trust in You, You will answer my cry for help and You will guide me through life's challenges. Help me to know You and to grow closer to You each day.

Thank You.

Amen.

Appendix
It's all about strategic leadership

In this appendix I would like to examine the benefits of looking at the transformation of a place through the lens of strategic leadership. If we are going to behave as one, follow the bigger picture and build differently, then having a strategic kingdom view of our place is vital. It's important to have a practical understanding of how our place is shaped and what can be done to bring about significant change.

I don't really want to create a generic model, as every place is different, but my hope is that this appendix will act as a very practical contribution to your local journey and perhaps inspire you to see how leadership plays its part in changing where you live.

What would happen in a place if *all* the 'strategic leaders' worked together, if they combined all their gifts, passion and resources for a single purpose – to see their place flourish and reach its full potential? What would happen if they didn't care who got the credit, but just focused on making their place better?

So what does a 'strategic leader' look like?

Although 'strategic leaders' can be described in many different ways (entrepreneurial, creative, activists, initiators, connectors, etc), I want to suggest five key qualities that I believe form the core of a 'strategic leader'. The dynamic nature of these qualities makes the people who carry these qualities significant agents of change.

- Pioneering
- Visionary
- Connecting
- Caring
- Mentoring

The qualities shown here are based on the ministry types listed in Ephesians 4:11: apostles (pioneers), prophets (visionaries), evangelists (connectors), shepherds (carers) and teachers (mentors). I believe these are the leadership characteristics that we find in those whom we refer to as 'strategic leaders'. I would also suggest that these are the qualities we see in leaders who have the capacity to create sustainable change. These qualities are also characteristics that we would wish to develop in emerging leaders who aspire to be 'strategic leaders'.

Who are the 'strategic leaders' within a place?

The strategic leadership within a city is the gateway to influence and the key to strategic (and sustainable) change. In any locality we can identify *four strategic leadership quarters*. It is within these quarters that we find our 'strategic leaders'.

These groups are *Church, Commercial, Civic* and *Community*. The groups are inextricably connected. Each of these leadership quarters contributes to influencing people and places. The lens through which we view a city is crucial to transformation. If we are to have the biggest impact in our place, we need to ensure that we focus on the areas where the shape of our place is being formed, and the narrative is being written.

What do the strategic leadership quarters look like?

Let's look specifically at the leadership quarters, and what is distinctive about each area.

- **Church leadership:** This includes all those who are part of the Church, including those who are involved in any form of Christian ministry or Christian charity. It can include church ministers, church officials, heads of Christian ministry or anyone who works or volunteers within the Christian Church.

- **Commercial leadership:** This includes all those who are involved in any form of business or profit-making corporation. It can include business owners as well as business directors, business managers, commercial networks, small business owners, entrepreneurs, etc.

- **Civic leadership:** This includes those who are involved in the statutory governance of a place. It can include elected officers, politicians, law enforcement and councillors, as well as those who are employed by the local authority or work within other statutory bodies.

- **Community leadership:** This includes those who work and volunteer within the local community. It can include residents' groups, heads of charities, health boards, social enterprises, councils for voluntary services, community action groups, other faith leaders, leaders of societies or pressure groups, etc.

We are not concerned with 'ring fencing' any particular area; in fact, overlap and interfacing is good. There will be those who have roles that cross multiple leadership quarters. Developing a portfolio of activities that grows and connects leaders in these quarters is the key to influence.

Who influences a place?

It's a fact that everything either flourishes or fails, depending on the leadership. Whether in a small organisation, or an entire city, leadership sets the culture. Get leadership right and everything else follows.

Whatever you may call your 'place' (a hamlet, village, town, city or borough), it defines to a certain extent your view of where you are. It sets up the lens by which you see your place, and it creates the boundaries of where you think your place might go in the future. For example, we believe that although not yet officially recognised through the British city status scheme, the significance of Doncaster, in terms of its population, infrastructure and national connectivity, justifies the use of the term 'city'. We believe that is where we are heading.

Within any place or locality, the culture is shaped by the key people of influence, the 'movers and shakers', as they are sometimes referred to. These 'movers and shakers' are those who are identified as the people (or groups of people) that make things happen. These 'influential leaders', for better or for worse, lead and shape a place. They may often share agendas, and sometimes they may not; either way, they will push a place in a certain direction, and they will most certainly set the narrative of a place.

How can leaders influence people and places?

Each of the leadership quarters has influence over a particular group of *people*, and is responsible for creating the narrative for that group. Some people groups may overlap across the quarters, but all will operate out of places.

Much has been written on the power of leadership to influence, motivate, provide direction and implement plans. Good leaders generally have the influence to transform positively; the 'groups' ultimately will take on the shape of those who lead them.

All the individuals within a group have a place out of which they live, work and operate. This is their *place*. We are referring here to specific geographical spaces, localities or regions.

It can sometimes be helpful to place people within common contexts to facilitate growth and synergy of need. Alan Macfarlane,[18] an anthropologist and historian, made a useful observation about the core needs of human society. Macfarlane identified four basic needs that are linked together. This can be a useful visual tool in linking the needs of people and places.

- **Meaning:** Everyone is looking for meaning, influence or relevance. In today's world, a church that can bring meaning and hope will lead the way in a place.

- **Control:** We live in a time when humanity feels out of control. Allowing people and communities to feel included in transformation provides much-needed buy-in.

---

[18] www.alanmacfarlane.com (accessed 23rd August 2018). Author's note: I have added to his original thought, and expanded. Every effort has been made to source the original material, but it cannot be located at this time.

- **Possessions:** Community assets are key to transforming places. There are areas of desolation in towns and cities up and down the land. Reclaiming these brings hope and life.

- **Friendship:** It's a fact that everyone is looking to belong to something. Families and friendships are vital in all we hope to achieve together.

There are a number of ways in which these geographical places can be identified. One way is to use the Local Government Boundary Commission for England mapping system;[19] another option may be to use the parish system.[20] All places have boundaries, and these are usually defined by the people in a place, and those who lead them.

Choosing an established boundary (or mapping system) has its advantages in terms of creating connections, statistics and understanding the geographical area out of which individuals live and work.

What about those who aren't leaders?

I like the terms 'Champions and Crowds' or 'Leaders and Legions'. Those who, when joined together, have the

---

[19] The Local Government Boundary Commission for England is responsible for conducting reviews of local authority electoral arrangements.

[20] A parish is a church territorial unit constituting a division within a diocese. A parish is under the pastoral care and clerical jurisdiction of a parish priest.

capacity to create momentum and change – these are our *crowds* or *legions*. The 'cultural spheres' (or 'seven mountains', as they are sometimes known) is an example of how our *crowds* or *legions* can be mobilised.[21]

The idea was developed by Bill Bright, who founded Campus Crusade, and Youth With a Mission founder Loren Cunningham, in 1975. Both men proposed that in order to transform a nation with the gospel, seven spheres of society must be reached. The spheres are often labelled business, government, media, arts and entertainment, education, family and religion. Health and sport are added into other models. Whatever groupings are used, the usefulness of the 'cultural spheres' model only really extends to support the evangelism, discipleship, prayer life and growth of individuals contained within those spheres. It collects and connects individuals together who have common needs and aspirations, and supports them in those needs and aspirations within specific spheres. This is no bad thing; after all, a city where the people of God are equipped for mission together, in all of their life, is a city where transformation and hope can flourish.

The 'cultural spheres' approach can provide momentum in a given area, but does not always translate into the strategic landscape of a place. The 'cultural spheres' is an activity-focused lens that does not easily connect with place leadership infrastructure (or the strategic leadership within a place). As such, the potential for place transformation will always be limited.

---

[21] https://www.generals.org/rpn/the-seven-mountains/ (accessed 21st August 2018).

Although there is some influence possible within the 'cultural spheres' model, the strategic leadership quarters within a place has more impact in creating the momentum needed for sustainable place transformation. There is an added advantage that the strategic leadership quarters model works regardless of place size or place demographic.

Call to action

In short, we need to start from where we are! Place transformation is not theory, it is practice, which is outworked daily through the lives of those who are motivated to care.

Make a start by gathering those you know in strategic leadership, and begin to answer these questions:

- Are you able to name the key leaders in each of the quarters within your place?

- If not, how would start to identify the key strategic leaders?

- Can you locate the relevant strategic plans currently being produced by your local authority?

- Do you have access to, and are you part of, the local networks and forums involved in creating strategy in your place?

- What portfolio of activities could you develop that would grow and connect leaders in each of the quarters where you live?

- How, where and with whom would you deliver these activities?

- Within your community, how can you identify the main needs of individuals and groups?

- Can you think how you might discover and connect with the aspirations of all those who live in your place?

- Are there any established boundaries already being used in your place?

- How could you use these place boundaries to identify specific groups of people and areas of interest?

This appendix is by no means complete – there is still work to be done; it is, however, intended to act as a contribution to the local transformation conversation.

Editor's note: The body of Christ

Sheila Jacobs

It's worth spending time reading and reflecting on 1 Corinthians 12. The Church is one body, with many different giftings and abilities. In short, we need each other:

> For just as the body is one and has many members, and all the members of the body, though many, are one body, so it is with Christ. For in one Spirit we were all baptized into one body – Jews or Greeks, slaves or free – and all were made to drink of one Spirit.
>
> For the body does not consist of one member but of many. If the foot should say, 'Because I am not a hand, I do not belong to the body', that would not make it any less a part of the body. And if the ear should say, 'Because I am not an eye, I do not belong to the body', that would not make it any less a part of the body. If the whole body were an eye, where would be the sense of hearing? If the whole body were an ear, where would be the sense of smell? But as it is, God arranged

the members in the body, each one of them, as he chose. If all were a single member, where would the body be? As it is, there are many parts, yet one body.

The eye cannot say to the hand, 'I have no need of you', nor again the head to the feet, 'I have no need of you.'
1 Corinthians 12:12-21

In this book, we have explored the need to work together in unity. Psalm 133 tells us, 'Behold, how good and pleasant it is when brothers dwell in unity! ... For there the LORD has commanded the blessing, life for evermore' (verses 1, 3). The message is clear: to receive God's blessing, we need to examine our thoughts and feelings about just how God views unity in His Church.

Jesus, in the Upper Room Discourse, prayed:

I do not ask for these [His disciples] only, but also for those who will believe in me through their word, that they may all be one, just as you, Father, are in me, and I in you, that they also may be in us, so that the world may believe that you have sent me. The glory that you have given me I have given to them, that they may be one even as we are one, I in them and you in me, that they may become perfectly one, so that the world may know that you sent me and loved them even as you loved me.
John 17:20-23

It seems that if we want to be an effective witness in the world, and invite many to join us on the journey as we follow our Lord Jesus, we need to take the call of unity very seriously. Perhaps we need to study the first chapters of Acts, too, and see the awesome things God accomplished through His unified body, as they lived together in very real harmony and strong fellowship. See for example Acts 2:42-47:

> They [the believers] devoted themselves to the apostles' teaching and to fellowship, to the breaking of bread and to prayer. Everyone was filled with awe at the many wonders and signs performed by the apostles. All the believers were together and had everything in common. They sold property and possessions to give to anyone who had need. Every day they continued to meet together in the temple courts. They broke bread in their homes and ate together with glad and sincere hearts, praising God and enjoying the favour of all the people. And the Lord added to their number daily those who were being saved.
> *(NIV)*

If we hope to influence our place, our family, our neighbours, our town, our country, for Christ, are we really brave enough to put our (often valid) differences aside, and work together as one for the kingdom? True, we may have very real differences in doctrinal interpretation, and may view some scriptures very differently from another denomination. But while we can't dismiss these issues out of hand, can we live with our differences, accepting that we don't always agree, but that we are still brothers and sisters in Christ?

Let's be aware when the enemy seeks to strike at the heart of Jesus' mandate, to sow disunity and divide us. We may not always agree on contentious issues, but we do need to bear with and forgive each other, and wholeheartedly follow our Saviour, loving each other as He loved us – 'in order that Satan might not outwit us. For we are not unaware of his schemes' (2 Corinthians 2:11, NIV). As the saying goes, we are all works in progress. But as we fix our eyes on Christ, we are the stronger for travelling together.

Call to action

Reviewing all that you have learned in this book, think about your own attitudes to unity. Be honest!

- What (or who) stops you?

- Identify fear! Are you afraid ... and why?

- How can you become more aware of the schemes of the enemy to hinder God's work in your place, especially regarding issues such as divisiveness? Are there people you can gather together to pray regularly for discernment and wisdom, breakthrough and encouragement?

- In what areas may you be able to move forward in your place? Who might you need to have a conversation with – today?

- Are *you* brave enough?

By thinking through these points, facing them in the light of Scripture, praying about and/or discussing them with a trusted Christian friend, group or leader, we pray that you see great kingdom encounters in your place as you shape and guide the lives of those you lead, those you influence, and those you love.

A final thought

from Alyson Mayer

Church of Jesus Christ: Are we rock or crazy paving?

How sad it is that the Church displays so much hurt caused by jealousies, gossip, assumptions, judgement, mistruth ... such a deviation from what we are called to be: the body of Christ, hope of the world. Often instead, the world is confused and even damaged by its pockets of division. 'Me and mine', a 'club' mentality, will never achieve what Christ set out as the blueprint for His Church.

I believe that when we surrender our agendas, our judgement and our prejudices, only then can we authentically refer to ourselves as the prepared Bride of Christ. Forgiveness, hope and *love* are what the people out there are looking for. So let's make sure the world sees the Church as a rock it can rely on, rather than as crazy paving!

Online resources

As part of the 'Call to action' sections in this book, Ian and Alyson are making available a range of free interactive materials and resources to support the ongoing conversation.

If you would like to find out more, please visit http://www.ianmayer.com/arewebraveenough/

or scan the code below.

See also:
www.twitter.com/5changes
www.facebook.com/5changes

Websites

Jubilee Trust:
www.jubileetrust.co.uk
www.twitter.com/jubileecloister

Jubilee is a Christian charity that works in partnership with individuals, groups and organisations, as well as through denominations, Christian networks and churches.

Manna Community:
www.manna.me.uk
www.twitter.com/mannadoncaster

Manna Community CIC is all about supporting people on life's journey. Manna manages a number of community buildings that have been configured to support its transformation work across communities. Manna's vision is to create a framework that can act as a context for meeting the broad range of physical, intellectual, emotional, social and spiritual needs within the local community.

About Ian and Alyson Mayer

Ian Mayer

Ian is an innovative entrepreneur who combines church, commercial, civic and community leadership to see influence and transformation. His key focus is about understanding people and how they behave in groups. Ian has successfully founded a number of virtual networks and virtual organisations. He currently manages a number of internet-based projects that range from business development to community and social networking.

As a trained teacher and graduate in technology, Ian has been involved in education and training since 1990. His roles have included teacher of design and technology and ICT, head of student services, head of marketing and director of information learning technology.

Ian first started working with internet and multimedia learning technologies in 1995. He is a member of Rotary, an organisation with more than a million members that is made up of influential leaders who come together to create positive and lasting change in communities and around the world.

www.twitter.com/ianrmayer

Alyson Mayer

Alyson is a dedicated people person who uses a range of technologies and social media to augment real-world relationships. Whether strategically, or at grass-roots level, her focus is about understanding and meeting the needs of individuals. She is passionate about investing in future generations, and sees Generation Y (also known as the Millennial Generation) as a strategic group in developing the physical, intellectual, emotional, social and spiritual needs of future communities.

Alyson currently manages a range of community projects and support services through a CIC, and has been involved in planting businesses since the early 1990s. She is also responsible for a range of Corporate Social Responsibility (CSR) policies which include reaching out to the charity, voluntary and community sector.

Alyson also operates a lifestyle consultancy service.

www.twitter.com/alysmayer